A Historical Guide
To Old Hill Village

Hill Historical Society
2014 Revision

HISTORICAL SKETCH OF HILL VILLAGE

The town now known as Hill emerged from a Masonian grant made in 1754 to a syndicate of men residing in Chester, NH. They gave this large 30,000 acre tract the name New Chester, but since the French and Indian War was in progress, the first permanent settler, Cutting Favor, did not arrive until 1765. Travelling by river he found this floodplain fertile and hospitable; no tree growth had to be removed to accommodate planting and grazing. And a small stream at the north end could power a mill to saw lumber and grind grain. Other settlers arrived in the time of the Revolution; Carr Huse on the floodplain by a brook near the southern end, and William Murray, Moses Dickerson and others farther from the river on the rugged highlands requiring heavy clearing of trees and rocks. By 1794 a ferry was in operation to connect with Sanbornton to the east, and by 1808 a toll bridge was in place as well as roads which were rapidly being laid out in all four directions.

The center of New Chester, a community made up of self-sufficient farms in the early 1800s, was above the river at the intersection of roads to Andover, Danbury and Alexandria. As the population grew, first the northern portion of the grant broke away as Bridgewater (1788) and later Bristol (1819) also to the north. The remaining part kept the name of New Chester until 1836, when the name was changed by the legislature to honor Governor Isaac Hill. It was at this time that New Chester (Hill) achieved its peak population in excess of 1300 people. In the first sixty years of settlement the hillsides would be largely cleared and tilled or in pasture. Today ubiquitous stonewalls stand in mute testimony of the herculean task involved.

But the days of the farm were coming to an end as word spread of the great fertile plains in the Midwest. Were it not for the availability of water power in the brooks tumbling down to the Pemigewasset, one cannot guess what might have remained, but Industrialization was coming to New England and water power and labor free of farm chores was its engine. Once again the floodplain gained favor as small industries located to take advantage of the water power of the Smith River and Mill Brook (later known as Needle Shop Brook). George Sumner and Frank R. Woodward emerged as the captains of industry in Hill, building factories, housing, social centers and stores. Indeed later Frank R. Woodward provided electric power and running water to the village long before these services were considered essential municipal services. As more and more people gravitated back to the floodplain, churches, schools and liveries sprang up and by 1848, when the Bristol Branch of the railroad was constructed through Hill, a thriving village was already there. There were soon a train station and two other flag stops in Hill, and in the early 1900s the Hill children rode the train daily to high school in Franklin. Meantime the automobile and the concomitant highways turned Hill's Main Street into a major route to the White Mountains, and a hotel and tourist cabins were built both for the travelers and destination tourists; Hill was renowned for Dr. Vail's Water Cure (Mary Baker Eddy was a frequent client). Also Woodward's glass cutter was the forerunner of the well known Red

Devil Industries of today. Nevertheless, Hill continued to lose population and by 1910 fewer than 600 people lived in Hill.

One might have questioned the wisdom of building a village on the floodplain of the Pemigewasset River, but Hill survived quite well. What floods occurred never fully inundated the village itself but frequently cut off the village from the north and the south for days at a time, and the bridge to Sanbornton frequently was destroyed by floods and ice jams. But ironically one hundred years after the town lost its name by an unexpected act of the state government in Concord, the federal government with the concurrence of the state government concluded that the village of Hill could be given up in the public interest, that is, for the welfare of the many downstream cities like Franklin, Concord, Manchester, Nashua, Lawrence and Lowell, which had been ravaged by the great floods of 1927, 1936, and 1938. And so in 1939 work began on the Franklin Falls flood control dam and the federal government purchased and then razed all but 14 of the buildings in Hill village in order that there would be no manmade debris in the impoundment area. The 14 buildings saved were moved to higher ground by a contractor using a railway and winch turned by horses. Only the steel bridge to Sanbornton remained and that was dismantled in 1952. Slowly the floodplain returned to meadow as Cutting Favor had found it nearly two centuries earlier. Indeed, for years the federal government leased the land back to local farmers for crops and pasture, but more recently vandalism discouraged these activities. Today, the old village site plays host to hunting, hiking, camping, and ski-mobiling. The Heritage Trail running along the Merrimack and Pemigewasset Rivers from Massachusetts to Canada passes through the old village. A comprehensive photographic history of the old village was published by the Hill Historical Society in 1991.

To their credit the townspeople decided to stay together and on their own initiative relocated to the heights just above and built a model planned community. At the time only 400 people remained, but today over 1,100 people live in Hill.

NOTE: In the following pages buildings mentioned are identified using the map numbers found in *Hill Village on the Pemigewasset* and the *Supplement* published by the Hill Historical Society.

LEGEND: Fourteen granite 4X4" posts have been set out at selected points in the old village site. These markers are indicated on the map segments as solid black squares with the appropriate letter, and the areas appearing in the accompanying photographs are outlined by two diverging dashed lines. Posts to mark points M and N are at and beyond the northern limits of the village.

MARKER A
GREENLEAF BLAKE HOUSE

The Blake house [#3] was built in 1819 by Colonel Ebenezer Webster, a relative of Daniel Webster. It was a two-storey, elegant colonial with Indian shutters and wide board floors. Located just north of the Franklin town line, it was a striking introduction to the Main Street of Hill for travelers going north. This house was moved to the *new* village and is located on New Chester Road.

Colonel Webster also operated a store [#8] across the street which was well known for its free-flowing hard liquor. In the 1850s, it became a cooperative store run by Division 341 of the New England Protectionist Union and later was moved northward on Main Street [#26]. In 1903, a house was built on the earlier store site, and this house (home of Jennie D. Blake) was also moved to the *new* village at the north end of New Chester Road.

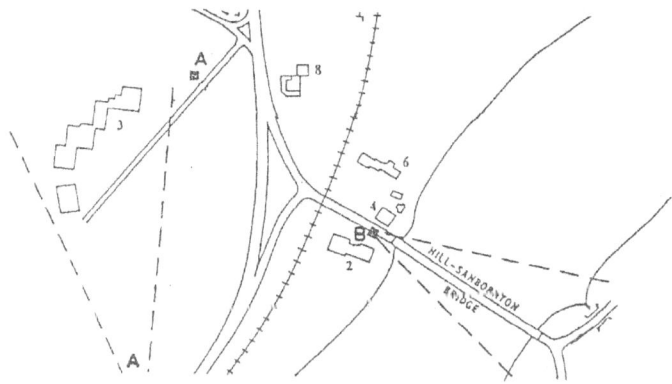

4

MARKER B
SANBORNTON BRIDGE

Four different bridges stood here over 145 years. The first bridge built in 1808, and was replaced in 1814 when it was carried off in a flood. The bridge was a privately owned toll bridge until 1860. In 1865, an ice jam lifted the bridge off its abutments and carried the bridge downstream. The third bridge was a double arch covered bridge, but it too was carried away in an ice jam in 1913. The fourth bridge was a steel truss bridge built on abutments 25 feet back from the former positions and seven feet higher with a raised center pier. This bridge remained after the town relocated (since it would not float during flood storage operations), but was sold for scrap in 1952.

Two houses [#2 &#4] near the bridge were owned by the company which owned, tolled and maintained the bridge. One house [#2] was moved to the *new* village on Mountain View Drive.

Elm trees lined Main Street (below) as seen from the bridge intersection.

MARKER C
LANE'S PRINT SHOP AND CAWLEY'S MILL

Roscoe Lane's print shop [#7] was on the west side of the street, where he printed town reports from 1896-1940. He was also known for his many photographs of the town and its people. This shop was moved to the *new* village and serves as the post office on Commerce Street. Many older houses, such as [#9 & #11], were large with sheds connecting to the barns.

Cawley's mill [near #A2] was located at the east end of Sawmill Road near the mouth of Mill Brook Mill Brook (later known as Needle Shop Brook) to capture the last bit of water power available. In the1870s this mill made oak felloes, the curved pieces of wagon wheels, which were shipped as far as San Francisco. The mill converted to steam power around 1900, but soon closed down when it became apparent that with steam power it was now more efficient to saw at the woodlot.

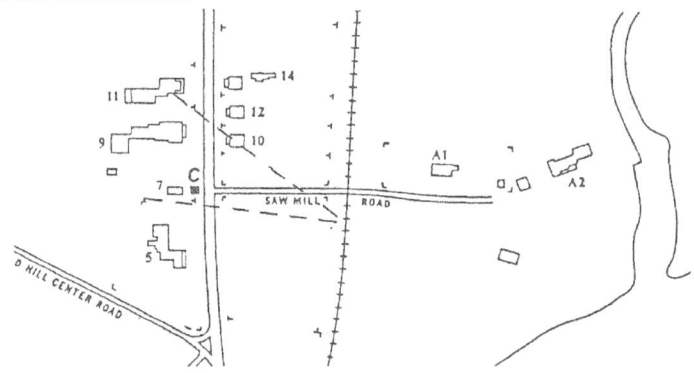

MARKER D
CHURCHES – A HOUSE DIVIDED

In 1885, Frank R. Woodward erected a building for a post office, store and hall to serve as a meeting place for the Hill Christian Society in which he was very active. He added an apartment block the next year, and the entire building was destroyed by fire in August 1887.

A month later the original church in the village burned down under suspicious circumstances (a fire was also set at Academy Hall [#41]). Woodward wrote a column in the *Merrimack Journal* implying that George Sumner was responsible for these fires. The ensuing libel suit divided the town and resulted in two churches being built as replacements. The Christian Church [#25], built in 1888, stood on the site of Woodward's Halls. The Congregational Church [#28] was built the same year on the east side of the street and a bit to the north.

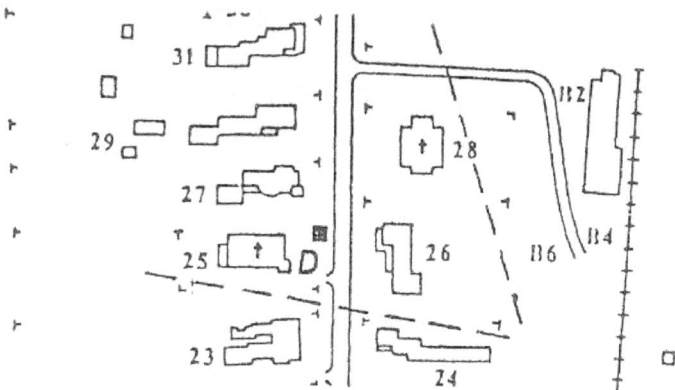

MARKER E
STORES AND SHOPS

Foster's (later Pearsons) grocery store [#29] was built in 1897. Further north on the west side of the street was Kimpton's drug store [#33] built in 1923 (relocated to New Chester Road in the *new* village).

On the east side to the north was Moses Little's store [#32] built in 1887. Opposite Kimpton's the Asa Prescott place [#30] built in 1788 was an early inn. In 1873, a large barn was added as a livery stable, which later became F.R. Woodward's Novelty Works when electric power freed manufacturing from Mill Brook Mill Brook (later known as Needle Shop Brook) and access to the railroad was needed for shipping orders.

East of Prescott's barn was Frank Foster's grain store [#B3] built in 1908. In 1915 gasolene was sold here and Hill had its first gas station. In 1919, Foster opened his garage and gas station [#34] on Main Street north of the site of Moses Little's store [#32].

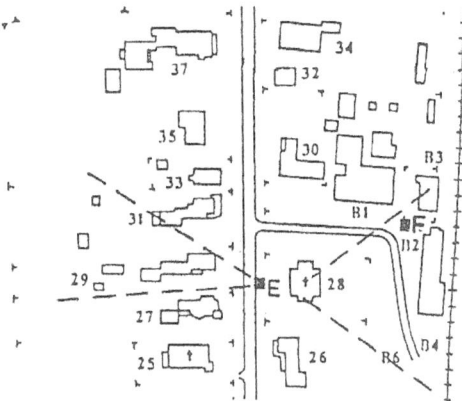

MARKER F
RAILROAD DEPOT

The railroad came to Hill in 1848 when the Bristol Branch was built from Franklin to Bristol. The station [#B2] was built six years later in 1854. At times the building also provided a grocery store, a post office, an ice cream parlor and an apartment for a section hand's family. The section house [#B4] to the south was used for supplies and tools to maintain the track. Across the road a storage house [#B6] was used by Pearsons store. In the 1870s it was reported that 3,000 cords of firewood were shipped from this depot to southern New England.

After 1936, when the railroad stopped service, the section house was used by the selectmen for an overnight lodging for "transient" people. This building was the first building relocated to the *new* village site and was used as an office by the State Planning & Development Commission. Later it was relocated near the town well on Cole's Flat.

The side street to the station was divided by a median upon which the Veterans monument was situated. The Veterans Monument is now located at the flagpole by the pond in the *new* village. Patriotic ceremonies continue to be held here.

9

Old Village Site Looking North From Mill (Needle Shop) Brook

Old Village Site Looking South From Mill (Needle Shop) Brook

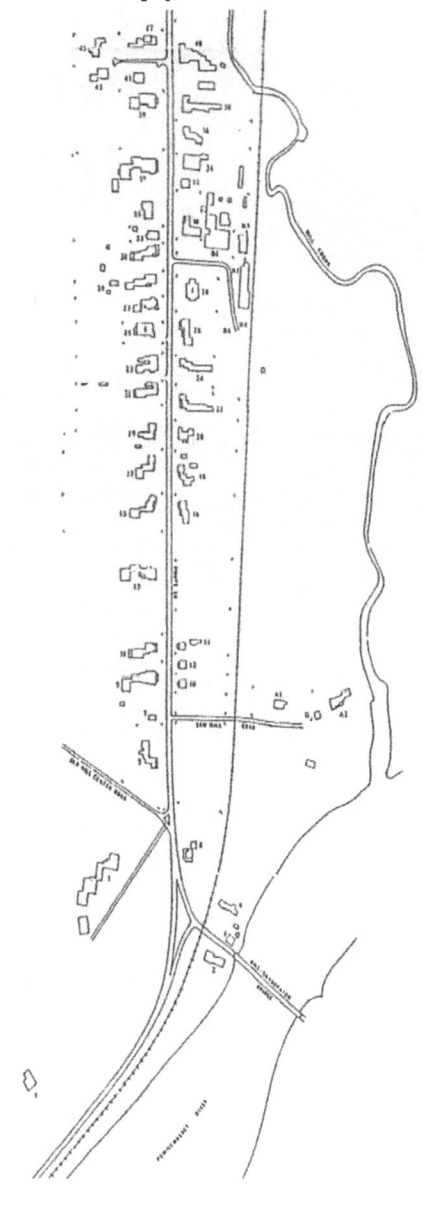

MARKER G
THE HOTEL – DR. VAILS WATER CURE

The hotel [#37] started as an Inn in the 1840s and in the 1860s was the home of Dr. William Vail's water cure (the spring still can be located in the present village near the ball field). The therapeutic waters attracted many people to Hill, including Mary Baker Eddy, the founder of Christian Science. The hotel was later converted to apartments.

Centrally located on the relatively flat stretch of Main Street, many came here on Saturdays to witness horse trotting races in the 1880s. Indeed horses and trainers came from surrounding towns. Wagers were made and refreshments were served at the hotel.

It is apparent from the sketch map that the older homes in the village were stately and generally connected to a barn by ells and sheds.

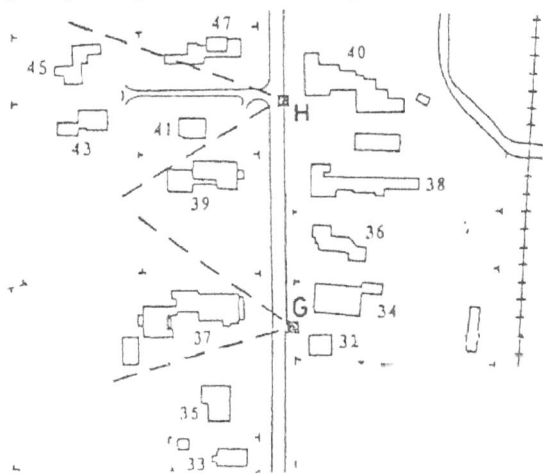

MARKER H
ACADEMY HALL

Set back from the street on the west side was the Academy Hall [#41]. Built in 1832 as the District #1 schoolhouse, it later housed the library and selectmen's office, and was used for town meetings after the new elementary school was built in 1909. Unknown persons attempted unsuccessfully to set it on fire in 1887. An elaborate town fountain with drinking water for human consumption at the top and for horses and pets at different levels below stood in front. The fountain was relocated to Commerce Street in the *new* village. Behind Academy Hall was a parsonage [#43] which also was moved to the *new* village.

Across the street in the 1840s was the Parker & Little store. In the 1870s, Woodward started his glass cutter business here, but moved it to Mill Hill after a fire. He replaced this shop with a large impressive house [#40] (below) in 1876 and lived there until his death in 1931.

MARKER I
CARR HUSE HOUSE

On this site stood the Huse house [#49] built in 1810 by Carr Huse, who was the second settler in the area (~1770). This property, which extended westward to Huse Mountain including the site of the present village, remained in the Huse family until 1941.

Harrison Morrill's blacksmith shop (later owned by Verne Straw) was located across from the Huse house for many years and was swept away in the Woodward dam failure in 1918. The "Mushroom" [#42] was built here in the 1920s, serving lunches and ice cream.

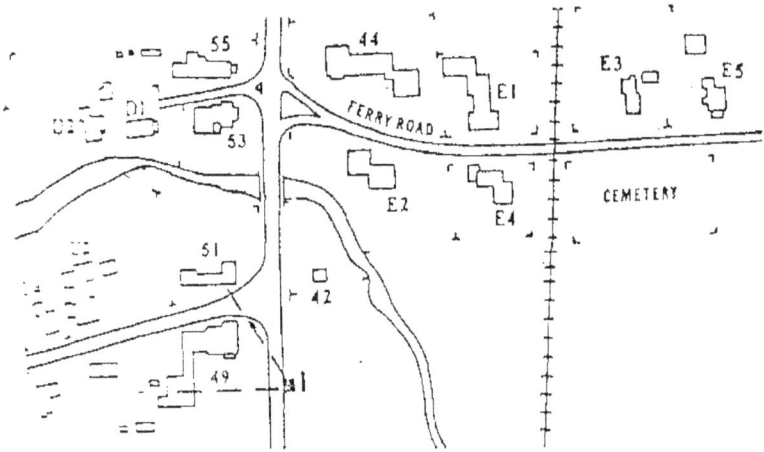

MARKER J
MILL HILL & WATER POWER

The availability of water power along Mill Brook Mill Brook (later known as Needle Shop Brook) was the earliest and most important factor in the emergence of a village in Hill as new shops and jobs attracted many away from farms. This mill site [#C8] was originally developed by Samuel Dearborn as a saw mill and later a grist mill. In 1872, Frank R. Woodward started manufacturing latch needles here for the knitting industry; but sold the site to G.H. Adams. Woodward movod upstream and built a new dam and shop [#C12] to make his famous glass cutter.

Houses for mill workers as well as several shops huddled on this steep slope until 1941. The road along the brook provided another link to Hill Center.

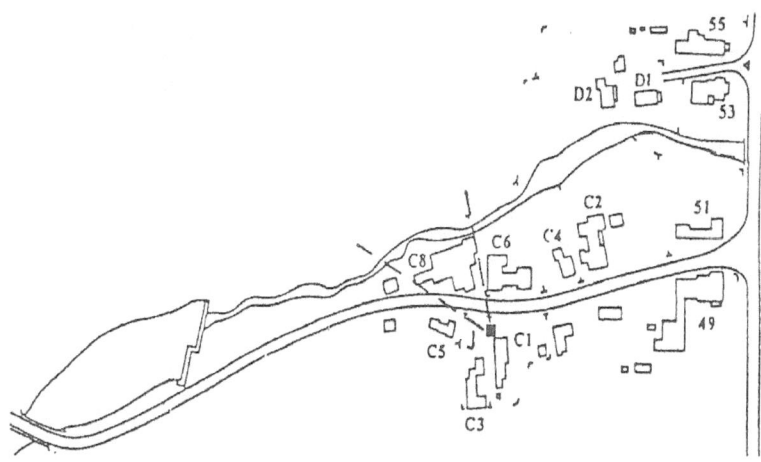

MARKER K
GEORGE SUMNER HOUSE

George Sumner, who came to New Chester in 1816, built a brick house [#44] here on the east side of Main Street in 1826. The road beside the house ran down past the cemetery to another ferry site.

Across the street Sumner had a carding shop which was carried away in a flood in 1824. The townsfolk took up a collection to help him rebuild.

Over the ensuing years several Industries occupied the two shop buildings on the west side of the street. Forbes Tannery & Carding Shop and later (in1874) the Williams & Eaton cabinet organ shop were in one [#D1]. John L. Mead Furniture and later carriages were repaired in the other [#D2].

Later #D1 was converted to apartments, and in 1918 tragedy struck this building. When the Woodward Dam on Mill (Needle Shop) Brook broke, #D1 was swept off its foundations and an elderly resident drowned. Rumors abounded that the Germans had sabotaged the dam.

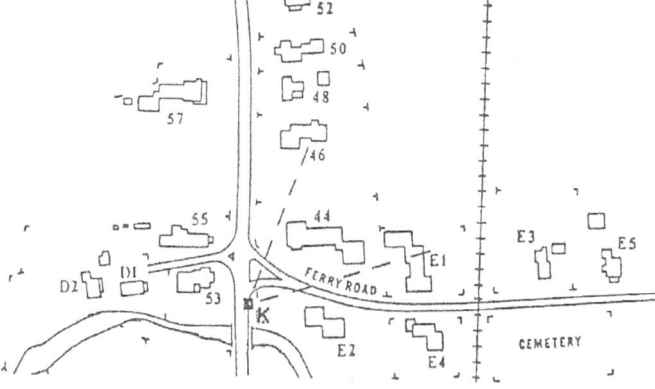

MARKER L
VILLAGE ELEMENTARY SCHOOL

In the early days there were ten or more school districts in Hill. Starting in 1813, school houses were built in several of these districts, which endured until the late 1800s when the districts began to be consolidated. In 1909, a substantially large schoolhouse [#61] was built on this site, and in 1910 the town reduced its school buildings to the one in Hill Center and this one in the village. The Hill Center School closed in 1923. The road beside the school, known as Sand Hill Road and later School Street, also was an early route to Hill Center.

Set back on the east side of the street was Dr. Fred Fowler's house [#54], part of which was built in 1785 and served as an inn and tavern in the early 1800s.

MARKER M
THE EDDY

Although there were several farms north of here, the Eddy marked the northern extent of the village. In the spring the high waters often built up here and separated Hill from Bristol for days at a time. Later the railroad would also be closed; and finally in 1936 the damage was so extensive that the railroad was never rebuilt. Since there was also low land south of the village which was inundated, residents frequently were forced to travel up Sand Hill Road and later Mill Hill Road to Hill Center to reach roads still open.

During one such flood Ernest Robie stalled his truck attempting to drive over a flooded section. He unloaded the oxen he was carrying and used them to pull the truck to higher ground!

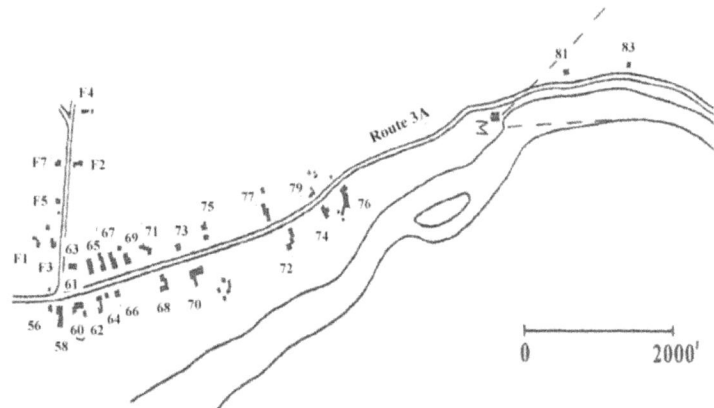

MARKER N
CUTTING FAVOR CABIN SITE

    Cutting Favor was the first English settler in this area, and having traveled by river he build his cabin here in 1766. He also established his mill on Dyer Brook nearby. His holdings extended a half mile along the river and one mile westward, as well as land across the river which he reached by ferry or by a ford at the north end of the island during low water.

    Greenloaf Blake built later [#78 & #80] in this area and continued the ferry (known as Blake's Ferry) well into the 1900s. The railroad whistle stop located here carried that name as well.

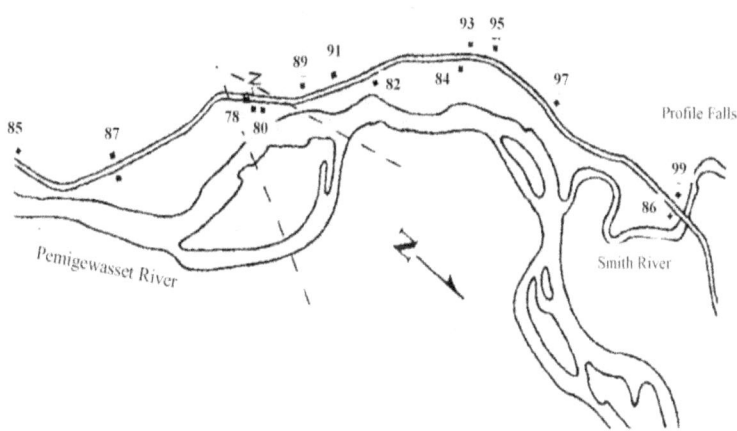

Christian Church built on land donated by Frank Woodward

Disaster from dam break

Roscoe Lane Print Shop became Post Office

Main Street looking West

Cutting Favor-Prescott-Wheeler house built in 1788 for Isaac Favor (1st white child born in New Chester)

Foster's Garage

Kimpton Pharmacy & Woodward Gas

New England Novelty
From Northwest

Verne Straw Blacksmith Shop

Steam Engine Crew

Train Entering Town
"Gulf Curve"

Hill/Sanbornton Bridge Over
The Pemigewasset

Aerial View of New Hill Village

Additional Publications

Hill Village on the Pemigewasset
In July, 1991 the Society published Hill Village on the Pemigewasset, a history of the old village. The book is in two parts: the first a narrative of the settlement of New Chester and the village built along the flood plain, and the second half depicting nearly every building in the flood plain, with as complete a history of the ownership and occupants of the houses as was possible.

The Story of Hill, New Hampshire, By Dan Stiles
The four years from 1939 through 1942 saw Hill Village selected for the site of a major federal flood control project. The people of Hill had to act to re-establish the village nearby. Dan Stiles, a noted journalist, recounted the amazing story for posterity in this very readable book of 72 pages liberally illustrated on 32 of those pages.

Our Chosen Place
This book is published in a soft cover, six-by-nine inches in size, containing over 300 pages of text, graphics and photographs and an index.

Part I of the book provides a 56-page narrative discussion of the past sixty-five years.

Part II of the book provides a two-page presentation of each home and building that was built in the New Village.

Hill Historical Society – PO Box 193, Hill, NH 03243
www.hillhistoricalsociety.com
hillhistoricalsociety@gmail.com